NATURE NOTES IV

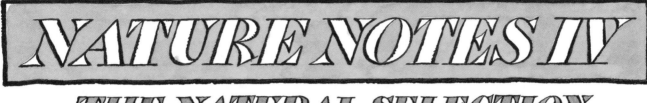

NATURE NOTES IV

THE NATURAL SELECTION

Peter Brookes

LITTLE, BROWN

A *Little, Brown* Book

These 'Nature Notes' cartoons first published in *The Times* between October 2001 and May 2004

First published in this collection in Great Britain in 2004 by Little, Brown

ISBN: 0 316 72722 9

Printed and bound in Italy

Little, Brown
An imprint of Time Warner Book Group UK
Brettenham House
Lancaster Place
London WC2E 7EN

www.twbg.co.uk

For Angela, Ben and Will

Osama bin Laden is held responsible for the September 11 attacks on America. US Special Forces stage their first ground raids in Afghanistan as the Taliban refuse to hand over bin Laden.

NATURE NOTES

Devil's Boletus
(Osama binladena) 💀

Highly poisonous fungus which shelters in dark, dank recesses (e.g. caves) making it difficult to locate. Its toxin is likely to provoke a violent reaction as it spreads through the body politic (see Fig.1). Also cf. Death Cap (*Talebanus terroris*).

Fig.1 A kick in the boletus.

N.B. The spore proliferates wildly.

Fig.2 Binned Laden

David Trimble's resignation as first minister of Northern Ireland in July puts pressure on the mainstream Republican movement, which now declares it has put some weapons 'beyond use'. Martin McGuinness and Gerry Adams call this step 'courageous'. Tony Blair joins the chorus of tributes to the Sinn Fein leadership for 'the boldness of this move'.

NATURE NOTES

On Being Sold a Pup

Fig. 1
Cosying up

Fig. 2
Piss process

All in bed together, this basketful of warm puppies presents such a delightful picture to the world. Completely disarming. Lavish care and attention on them *(see Fig. 1)*, acceding to their every demand, and eventually they will repay you handsomely in kind *(see Fig 2)*.

The Prime Minister visits Saudi Arabia, Syria, Jordan, Israel and the Palestinian Authority to bolster support for the international coalition against terrorism. The value of his mission is questioned: there are few signs of concrete progress and he receives several embarrassing public dressings-down from leaders he meets, notably from Syria's President Assad on the issues of terrorism and the Middle East peace process.

Tony Blair's support for the US action in Afghanistan continues, unwavering.

After a tumultuous year for Blair he remains at the helm of his party, despite rumours of successors-in-waiting. Iain Duncan Smith and Charles Kennedy cling on too, though IDS's leadership is thrown into fresh turmoil when former Tory cabinet minister Michael Heseltine calls for his sacking.

NATURE NOTES

Party Fare
Your critical guide to getting
the bird this Christmas.

The Famous Grouse
(*Numero duo*)
Not yet the premier
choice. Plump but
bitter and
sour.

Quail
(*Liberalis minimalis*)
Tiny and
insubstantial.
No meat on the
bone. No bone.

ONE PENNY 1

To scale

Brace of Pheasant (*Toryus reductio*)
Completely shot at. No discernible flavour.

22 xii 07
Peter Brookes

A row over the alleged neglect of a 94-year-old NHS patient degenerates into a personal battle between Tony Blair and Iain Duncan Smith, who accuses the government of lying about the case. The Tories claim the affair is an illustration of the appalling state of the NHS under Labour.

NATURE NOTES

Skunk
(Duncus skunkus)

Preys on easy targets like dead ducks (*Healthus serviceus*). If in turn it is attacked, it will create an almighty stink of stomach-churning nauseousness. With its tail up, the anal glands activate and this obnoxious little rodent soon finds itself in bad odour.

Fig.1 Related to the Chingford semi-housetrained polecat *(q.v.)*.

Zimbabwean President Robert Mugabe launches the campaign for his presidential election, saying the country faces 'political war' with former colonial ruler Britain.

Not recommended for breakfast.

NATURE NOTES

African Python
(Mugaba tophanana)

Egg-laying creep which will go to great lengths (reportedly up to 23ft) in crushing all opposition. Victims are turned over, swallowed whole, and left to stew in their own juice. All so unpalatable.

Fig.1
Going down a treat in Harare.

2 ii 02
Peter Brookes

Transport Secretary Stephen Byers' struggles are protracted (like this caption). In March 2000 he is implicated in the near collapse of Rover when BMW sells the company. In October 2001 he puts Railtrack into administration; two days later Jo Moore's infamous memo is leaked. She is backed by Byers and does not resign. In January 2002 he is on holiday during rail strikes, prompting outrage in some newspapers, and a month later Ms Moore is back in the spotlight after claims she proposed bad news be released on the day of Princess Margaret's funeral. Finally Byers announces the resignations of Ms Moore and transport press chief Martin Sixsmith, who denies he has resigned. Railtrack then begins court action against the beleaguered Byers. He subsequently admits in an interview with Jonathan Dimbleby that the state of public transport in Britain is not good enough.

Crufts week. Blair is teased about his penchant for designer clothes and is taunted for his unwavering loyalty to Bush, as hawkish pronouncements about toppling Saddam Hussein's regime continue to emanate from the White House.

NATURE NOTES

Toy Poodle
(*Canineus supineus*)

Fig. 1
Taking a lead

Coat and cuffs
by Paul Smith.

Fig. 2 Steel-capped boot

Voted Best of Breed (Brown-nosed Division), Crufts 1998, 1999, 2000, 2001 and 2002. Intensely loyal despite occasional abuse (*see Fig. 2*). A Pedigree Chump.

Palestinian leader Yasser Arafat makes a statement condemning terrorist acts that target civilians, following a suicide attack in Jerusalem. It comes hours after Israeli forces make new incursions into Palestinian territory on the West Bank.

Jean–Marie Le Pen stuns France by his success in the first round of the French elections, as he shafts the ineffectual French Left led by Lionel Jospin. Tens of thousands of people take part in demonstrations, meaning certain victory for Jacques Chirac in the final round.

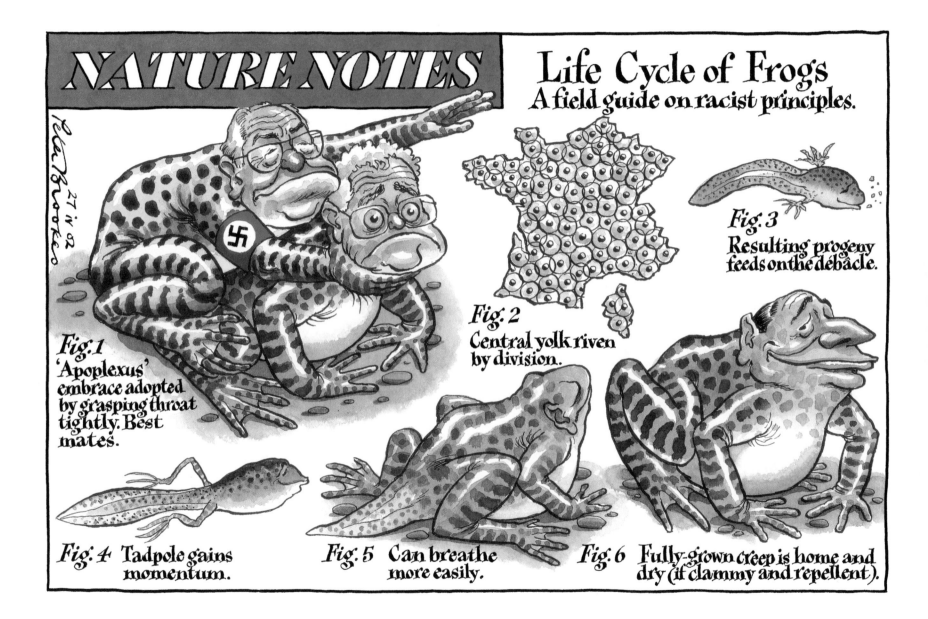

NATURE NOTES

Life Cycle of Frogs
A field guide on racist principles.

Fig.1 'Apoplexus' embrace adopted by grasping throat tightly. Best mates.

Fig. 2 Central yolk riven by division.

Fig. 3 Resulting progeny feeds on the débâcle.

Fig. 4 Tadpole gains momentum.

Fig. 5 Can breathe more easily.

Fig. 6 Fully-grown creep is home and dry (if clammy and repellent).

English local elections. A mixed night leaves Labour, the Conservatives and the Liberal Democrats with little to celebrate. Labour loses some ground and the Conservatives fail to get the clear breakthrough for which they had hoped. The British National Party triumph in Burnley. A monkey is elected as mayor of Hartlepool . . .

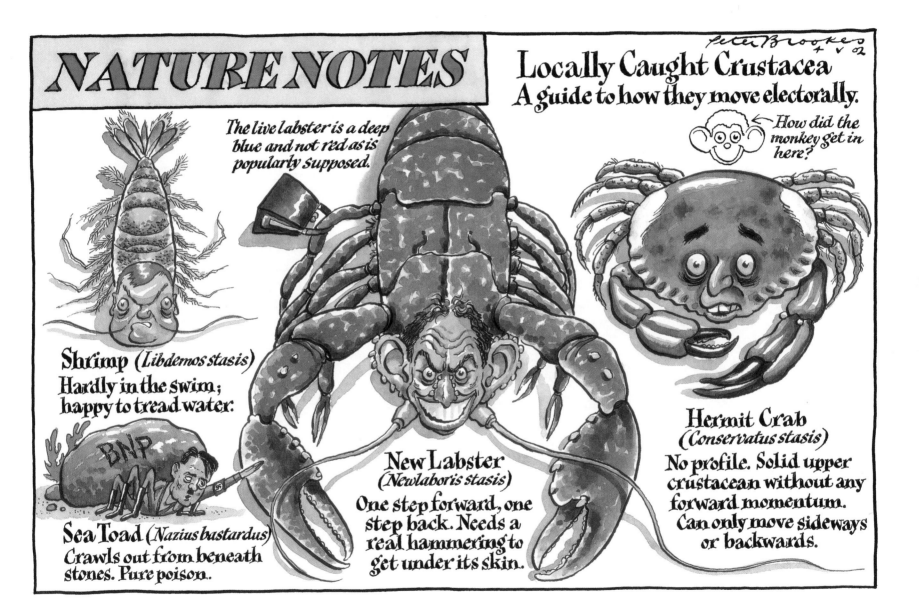

NATURE NOTES

Locally Caught Crustacea
A guide to how they move electorally.

How did the monkey get in here?

The live labster is a deep blue and not red as is popularly supposed.

Shrimp (*Libdemos stasis*)
Hardly in the swim; happy to tread water.

Sea Toad (*Nazius bastardus*)
Crawls out from beneath stones. Pure poison.

BNP

New Labster
(*Newlaboris stasis*)
One step forward, one step back. Needs a real hammering to get under its skin.

Hermit Crab
(*Conservatus stasis*)
No profile. Solid upper crustacean without any forward momentum. Can only move sideways or backwards.

A parade of Westminster nuts: from Cherie Blair, whose comments about young Palestinians feeling they have 'no hope' but to blow themselves up do not go down well in Westminster, to Telecoms giant Vodafone, who boldly defy hard-hit shareholders by handing £2.42 million to chief executive Sir Christopher Gent during a period in which the company has racked up the largest loss in UK corporate history.

NATURE NOTES

Mixed Nuts and Nutcases
A further selection from the Westminster and City jungles.

Not-so-Sweet Chestnut
(Terrorista sympatico)

Monkey-Nuts
(Media anathema)

Backs-to-the Walnut
(Honeymoonus isoverus)

Cash-ew Nut
(Vodafonus obscenebonus)

Brazil Nut *
(Samba victoria)
* for obvious reasons, currently out of favour.

Mayor of London Ken Livingstone loses his temper at a party after being told his pregnant girlfriend has been smoking. Livingstone is accused of being drunk. The Metropolitan Police decline to press charges, despite reports of an additional 'scuffle' with another party guest.

David Blunkett stands by controversial plans to re-classify cannabis as a less harmful drug. The move comes in for fierce criticism from the Conservatives and some Labour backbenchers, who say it will send out a confusing message to young people and encourage drug use.

NATURE NOTES

Peter Brookes
13 vii 02

Kite
(Blunkus skunkus)

Nothing is as mind-blowing or liberating as being as high as a kite. But confusion can set in, and the kite can easily fly round and round in ever-decreasing circles until it spins itself up its own fine-feathered sphincter. Far out, man.

Fig: 1
Skunk provides a wonderfully noxious high.

Union leaders and left-wing Labour MPs protest against the privatisation of public services at a conference on Saturday. Blair shores up the coalition with support from Italy's Prime Minister Silvio Berlusconi.

Iraq offers to re-open dialogue with United Nations weapons inspectors. Secretary of State Colin Powell and President George Bush dismiss the offer but UN Secretary General Kofi Annan gives a cautious welcome to Saddam Hussein's invitation for the chief inspector, Hans Blix, to visit Baghdad for 'technical talks'.

Delegates at the World Summit on Sustainable Development in Johannesburg enjoy nightly banquets in a luxury purpose-built conference centre metres from some of Johannesburg's worst slums. Deputy Leader John Prescott arrives just in time to call for action to provide clean drinking water to the world's poorest people.

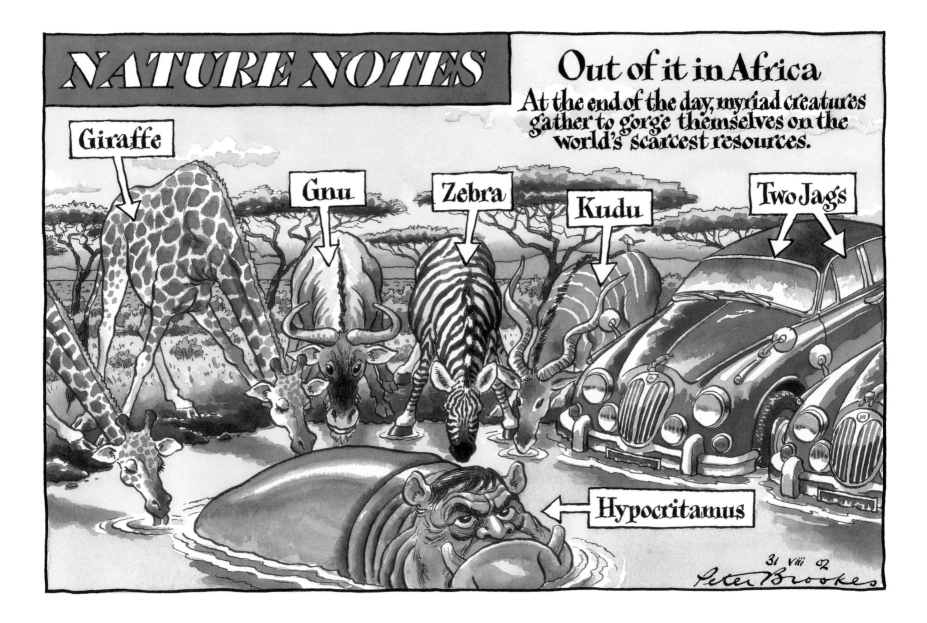

US Vice President Dick Cheney – one of Washington's leading hawks – makes it clear in his strongest speech to date that he backs military action against Iraq. It is reported that his speech is 'off message' and has not been vetted by Bush.

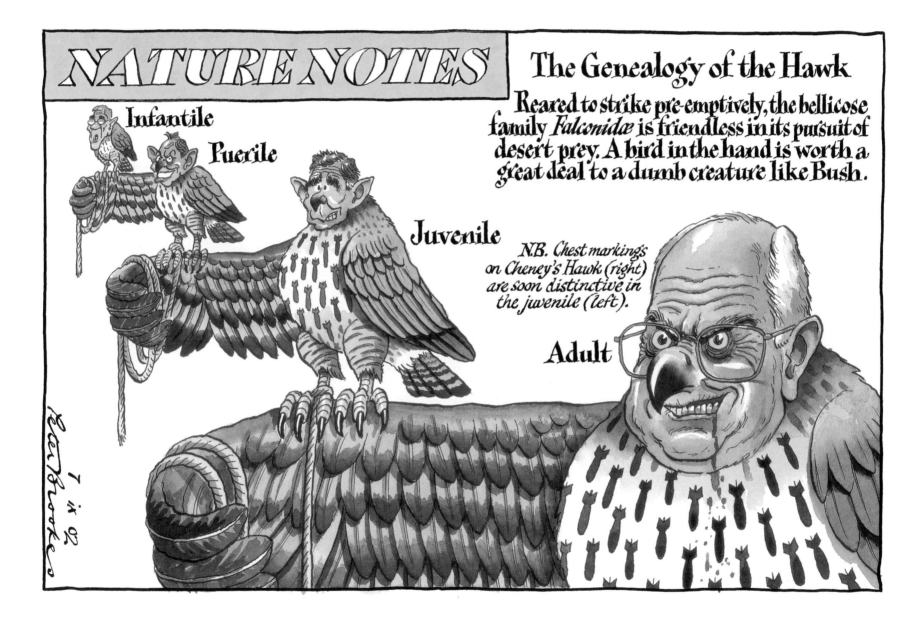

NATURE NOTES

The Genealogy of the Hawk

Reared to strike pre-emptively, the bellicose family *Falconidæ* is friendless in its pursuit of desert prey. A bird in the hand is worth a great deal to a dumb creature like Bush.

Infantile

Puerile

Juvenile

N.B. Chest markings on Cheney's Hawk (right) are soon distinctive in the juvenile (left).

Adult

After a year as leader of the Tory party Iain Duncan Smith faces accusations that no one is noticing them. Former Tory press chief Amanda Platell says she cannot see 'any chance' of the party winning the next election under Duncan Smith.

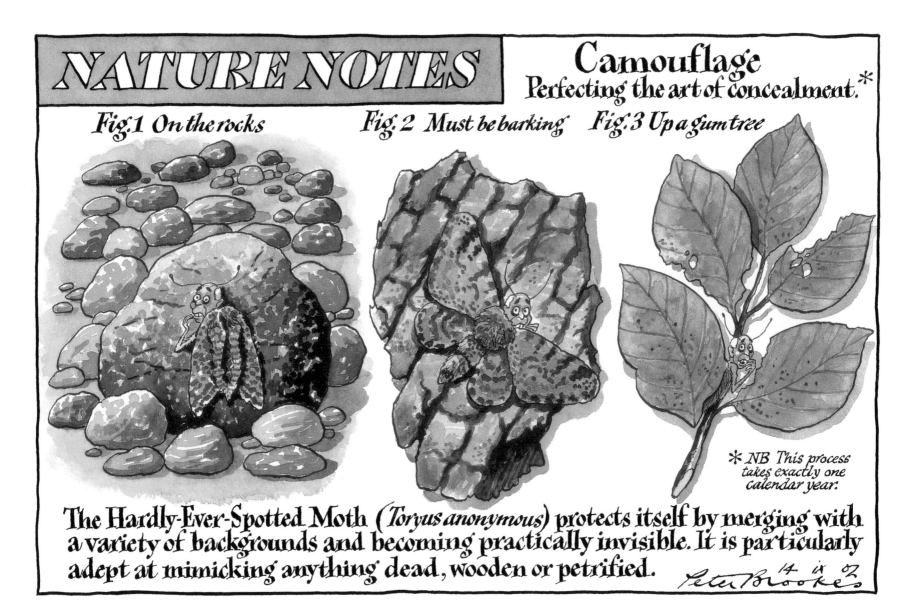

NATURE NOTES

Camouflage
Perfecting the art of concealment.*

Fig. 1 On the rocks   **Fig. 2** Must be barking   **Fig. 3** Up a gum tree

* NB This process takes exactly one calendar year.

The Hardly-Ever-Spotted Moth (*Toryus anonymous*) protects itself by merging with a variety of backgrounds and becoming practically invisible. It is particularly adept at mimicking anything dead, wooden or petrified.

The Prince of Wales is embroiled in a row over his private communications with government officials. It is claimed that Lord Irvine, the Lord Chancellor, has complained after being 'bombarded' with missives from the Prince outlining his concerns on 'compensation culture'. He is also alleged to have said, in private discussions with a senior politician, that if the government banned hunting he might as well leave the country and spend the rest of his life skiing.

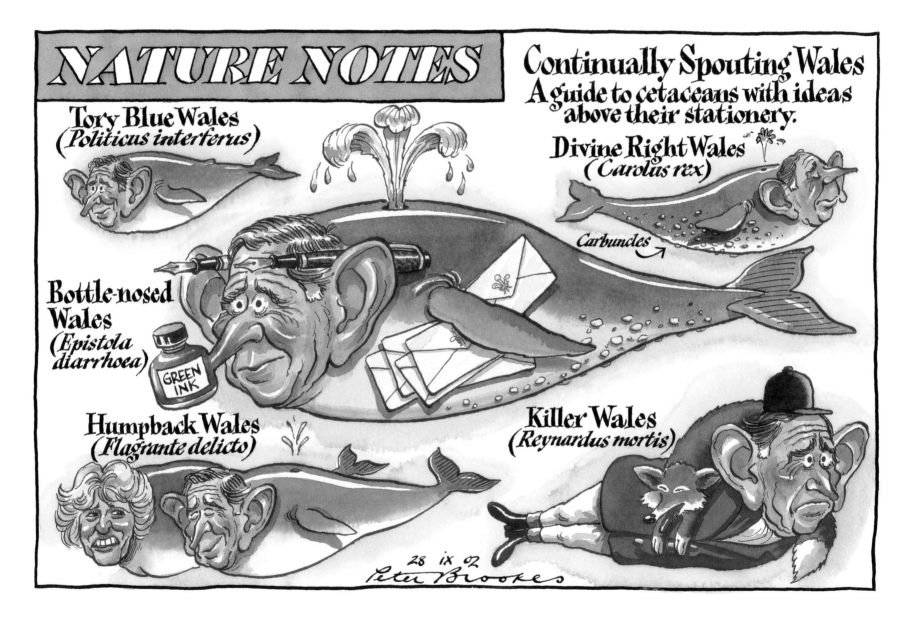

Education Secretary Estelle Morris resigns to tears and applause after saying the job was too important to have 'second best'. She claims she feels that she has not been as effective in the cabinet post as in her old job as schools standards minister. She has also found the media intrusive – Whitehall insiders say the last straw was being told she needed a makeover because of criticism of her dress sense.

NATURE NOTES

An Apple for the Teacher

Variety : Saint Estelle

Taste : Saccharine sweet, but with more than a hint of bitterness if wrapped in newsprint. Loses its taste in a cold climate.

Texture : When it comes to the crunch, this thin-skinned variety disappoints. Store on a high shelf for future use.

Recipe for disaster : All cut-up and stewed, makes a spectacular crumble.

Fig.1
Spectacular
crumble

NB Saint Estelle
bruises easily, so
handle with care.

Peter Brookes 26 X 02

France postpones an Anglo-French summit following a row between Jacques Chirac and Tony Blair over proposed reforms to the Common Agricultural Policy. It is reported that Blair has been outmanoeuvred by Chirac and German Chancellor Gerhard Schroeder, who have made a deal to limit CAP subsidies to EU farmers.

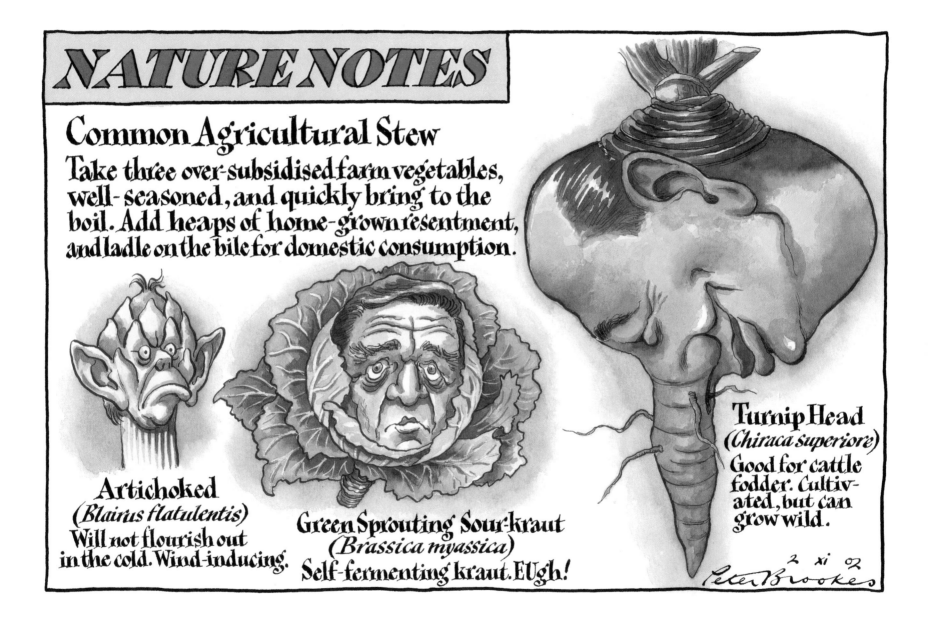

NATURE NOTES

Common Agricultural Stew

Take three over-subsidised farm vegetables, well-seasoned, and quickly bring to the boil. Add heaps of home-grown resentment, and ladle on the bile for domestic consumption.

Artichoked
(*Blairus flatulentis*)
Will not flourish out in the cold. Wind-inducing.

Green Sprouting Sour-kraut
(*Brassica myassica*)
Self-fermenting kraut. EUgh!

Turnip Head
(*Chiraca superiore*)
Good for cattle fodder. Cultivated, but can grow wild.

2 xi 02
Peter Brookes

Sir Michael Peat's investigation into the collapse of the trial of former royal butler Paul Burrell unearths an allegation made by a former servant about an incident involving Prince Charles and his ex-valet, Michael Fawcett. Subsequently the prince's former deputy private secretary Mark Bolland alleges in the *News of the World* that Peat once asked him whether the Prince was bisexual.

The Fire Brigade begin an eight-day strike, as their union leader Andy Gilchrist demands a 16% payrise for his workers. Gordon Brown calls the demands 'unaffordable'. Tube staff are sent home without pay for refusing to work during the strike because of safety concerns; Aslef, the drivers' union, say if disciplinary action is taken against the drivers it will be 'in dispute' with London Underground and Bob Crow, General Secretary of the Rail Maritime and Transport union, accuses LU of breaking the law.

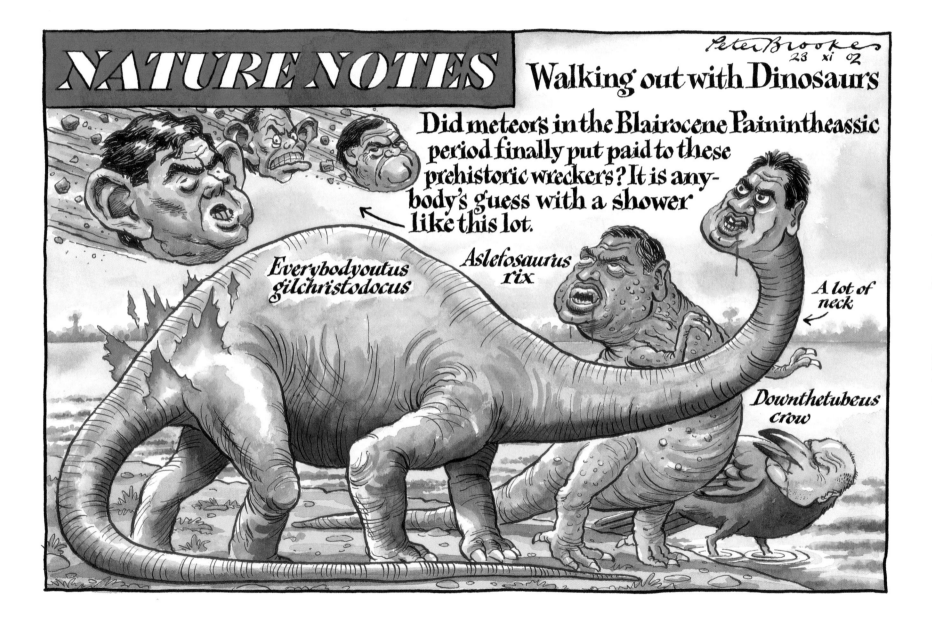

Despite forecasts of economic growth earlier in the year, it is reported that a sluggish economy and worsening public finances are likely to be the downbeat themes of Gordon Brown's pre-budget report. The abandonment of Prudence is confirmed when Brown announces government borrowing will almost double to £20 billion – a higher figure than in any year since Labour came to power.

NATURE NOTES

Horny (or Brown) Owl
(Prudenceis dumpeda)

Fig:1

Fig:2

PRUDENCE

PRUDENCE

In a harsh climate there is a disinclination to mate, and the Horny Owl considers it would be a twit to woo. In fact, it couldn't give two hoots (less tax) for its *inamorata*.

Peter Brookes 30 XI 02

Cherie Blair faces public embarrassment when it emerges she has bought two flats in Bristol with the aid of convicted fraudster Peter Foster, boyfriend of her friend and lifestyle guru Carole Caplin. The *Daily Mail* subsequently publishes a series of emails that show Foster also offered Cherie the use of his accountant, who is due to stand trial on fraud charges.

The Bush–Blair alliance on the War against Terror holds strong. US officials say troops are being sent to Kuwait to prepare for action against Saddam Hussein. Blair tells UK armed forces they too must be ready for a possible confrontation with Iraq.

America continues to press for military action in Iraq, despite the United Nations Secretary General Kofi Annan's calls for weapons inspections to be allowed to continue.

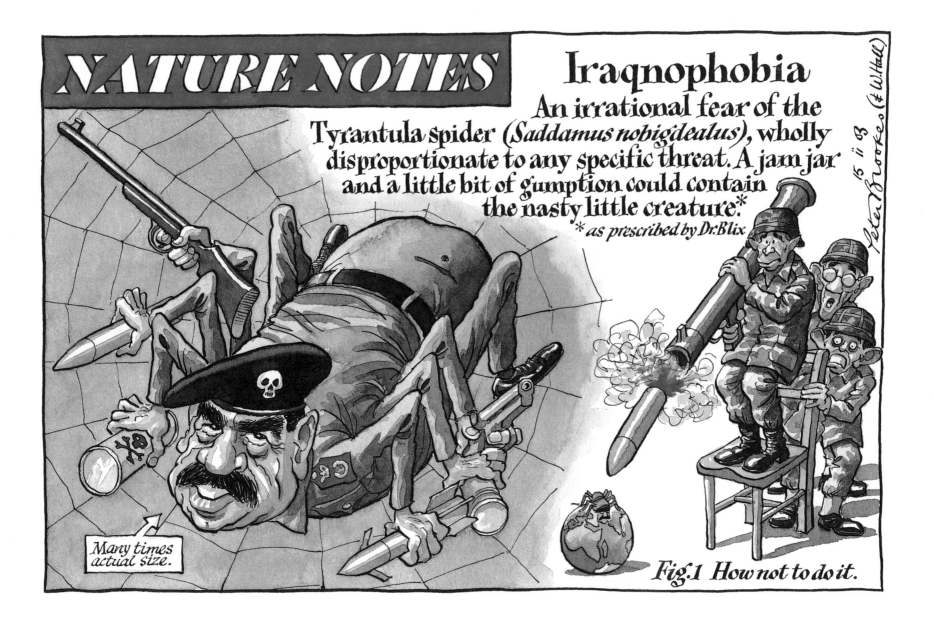

Another Crufts week (this year it is the 100th show). The coalition of countries in favour of war stands firm but diplomacy rumbles on as Blair drives for a second UN resolution to win over public opinion in the UK.

The US has no such qualms. Defence Secretary Donald Rumsfeld continues to air the possibility that the country will go into battle with or without the support of the UN. He triggers fury in France and Germany after he dismisses their opposition, calling them part of 'old Europe'.

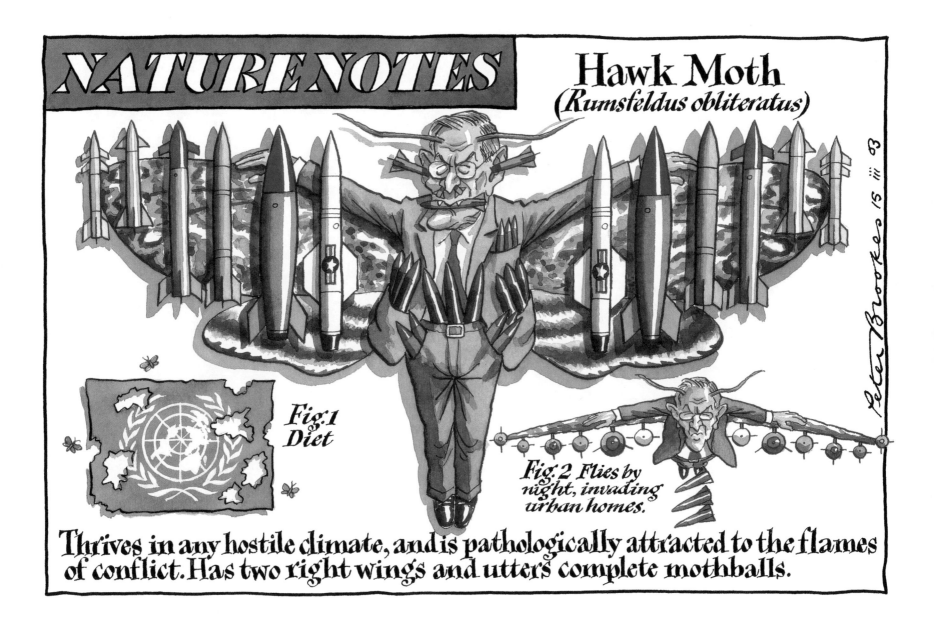

NATURE NOTES

Hawk Moth
(Rumsfeldus obliteratus)

Peter Brookes 15 iii 03

Fig.1 Diet

Fig.2 Flies by night, invading urban homes.

Thrives in any hostile climate, and is pathologically attracted to the flames of conflict. Has two right wings and utters complete mothballs.

War breaks out on 20 March. As US intelligence officials try to determine whether Saddam Hussein was killed or injured by US pre-dawn air strikes on Baghdad, United States and British forces launch aerial assaults on targets in Baghdad and beyond. Bombs rain down on the Iraqi capital, as the US unleash its 'shock and awe' strategy.

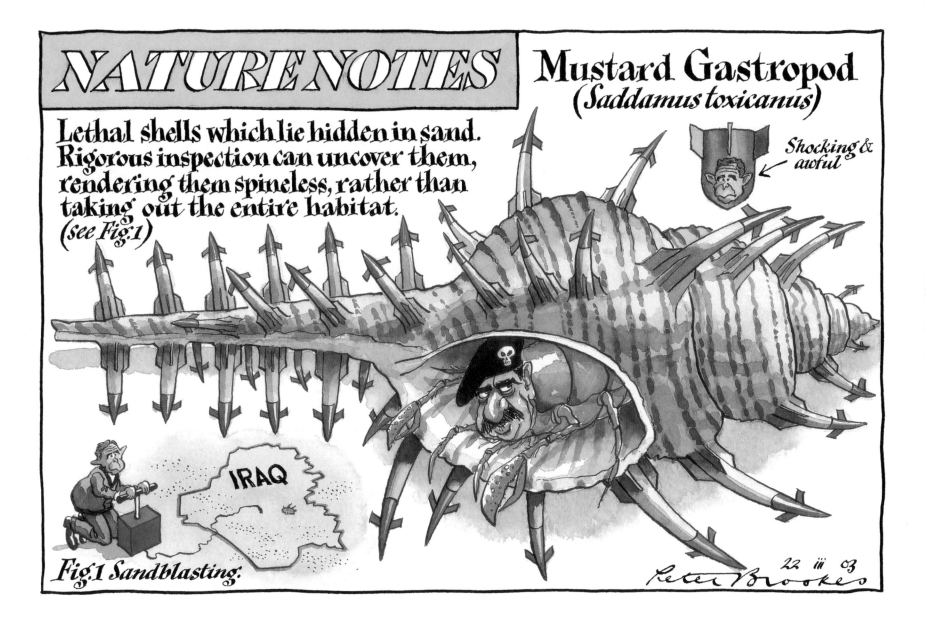

At the end of a trip by Tony Blair to the US, which includes a Camp David summit with George Bush, Blair reiterates his support for America and his belief in the war.

Baghdad falls. Russia, France and Germany insist that the UN have a leading role in shaping Iraq in the post-conflict era. The United States makes it clear it is unlikely to hand control over to the UN in the immediate future. Blair's attempts to bridge the ever-widening gap between America and Europe do nothing to broach an entente.

NATURE NOTES

Shoebill
(Slipper slapperus)

The fractious shoebill is so-named because of its habit of footwear assault, a most extreme form of insult and, ultimately, sole-destroying.

Clare Short resigns, calling for an 'elegant succession' to the Labour leadership, by which she means Gordon Brown. Blair continues to face opposition from the Left, most vocally from ex-Cabinet ministers Frank Dobson and Robin Cook, and former culture secretary Chris Smith, who announces he is to leave Parliament at the next election after a twenty-year stint as an MP.

Tony Blair embarks on a visit to the Gulf as the row begins to flare up about the coalition's failure to find Iraq's alleged weapons of mass destruction.

The government botches its announcement of sweeping changes to the legal system. Cabinet newcomer Lord Falconer, an old friend of Blair's, will head a new department of constitutional affairs. Lord Falconer has never been elected and was promoted to the Lords soon after Labour came to power in 1997.

Tony Blair is under pressure to raise directly with George Bush the case of British prisoners in Guantanamo Bay in Cuba. Charles Kennedy's comments reflect many views: 'I think a special relationship or that degree of influence has to be a two-way street. What we seem to be encountering at this stage is very much one-way traffic.'

NATURE NOTES

Large Red, White and Blue
(Blairus americanus)

On capture this species raises barely an audible squeak in protest. Bright coloration makes it an obvious prey for predators on the greenery of the backbenches. Displayed in supine aspect.

Fig.1 Weapon of moth destruction

Distribution

12 Vii 03
Peter Brookes

Iain Duncan Smith continues to miss opportunities to attack the government, which is being closely scrutinised over the handling of intelligence in the run-up to the war, as the Hutton Inquiry into the death of weapons expert Dr David Kelly reaches its closing stages.

NATURE NOTES

Three-toed Sloth (*Torius torporus*)

While its enemies destroy themselves in the Hutton jungle, the sloth chooses to hang upside down in a lethargic stupor, doing absolutely nothing and going nowhere. Fast.

6 ix 03
Peter Brookes

Fig.1 Do not underestimate the termination of a quiet mammal.

Iain Duncan Smith launches a savage attack on the Prime Minister in his keynote speech to the Conservative conference as part of a fightback against his Tory critics. He accuses Blair of leading a 'deceitful, incompetent, shameful and lying government'. The highly personal attack is not generally seen to be a wise move.

Scepticism at IDS's ability to lead the Tories continues at Westminster. Party chief whip David Maclean denies reports he told Duncan Smith he had lost the confidence of MPs, but there are speculations that plotting will shortly break out into open mutiny.

Sure enough, three weeks later Iain Duncan Smith is ousted after failing to win a vote of confidence from his party. Michael Howard looks increasingly likely to become the next Tory leader.

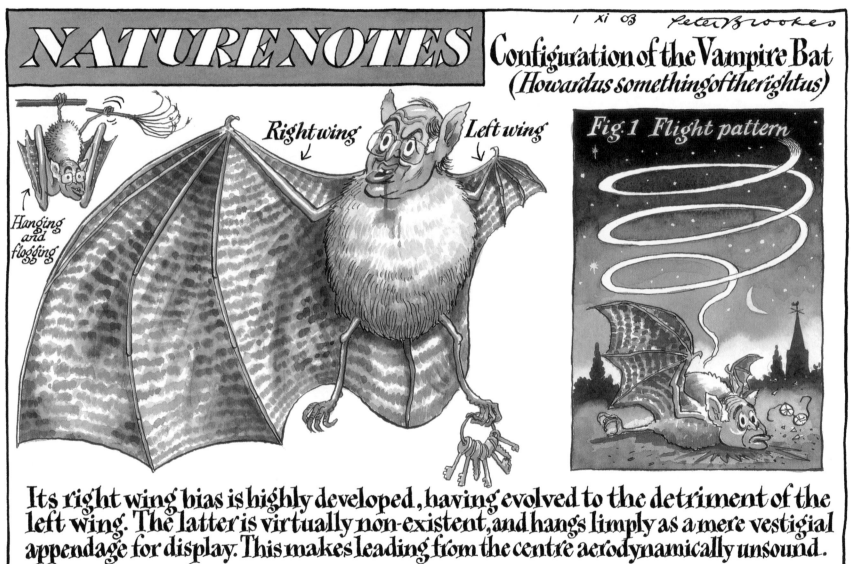

NATURE NOTES

Configuration of the Vampire Bat
(Howardus somethingoftherightus)

1 xi 03 Peter Brookes

Hanging and flogging

Right wing

Left wing

Fig. 1 Flight pattern

Its right wing bias is highly developed, having evolved to the detriment of the left wing. The latter is virtually non-existent, and hangs limply as a mere vestigial appendage for display. This makes leading from the centre aerodynamically unsound.

Gordon Brown admits he asked Blair to grant him membership of the National Executive Committee – Labour's ruling body – and was turned down. Private tension between Blair and Brown appears to boil over in public after a dinner between the two, which is compared to the infamous 1994 meeting at the Granita restaurant in Islington. There are suggestions that Mr Brown particularly wants to be on the NEC because he is worried about former cabinet minister Peter Mandelson's increasing influence over election planning.

NATURE NOTES

8 xi 03 Peter Brookes

The Brown Blair
(*Granita dyspepsia*)

A diet of Islingtonian sun-dried tomatoes and rabbit polenta results in grizzly brown blairs suffering indigestion and experiencing an excrutiating pain in the a*se. Talk about a bum deal...

Fig.1 Patent 'Mandy' trap

Claws 4

Fig. 2

GORDIE

NEC

Who's been sitting in MY chair?

Michael Howard makes his mark within his first fortnight as leader of the Tory party, achieving – as some commentators put it – more in ten days than IDS did in 100. He effectively challenges Tony Blair at *Prime Minister's Questions* and even spikes jibes about his Dracula image by poking fun at it himself.

NATURE NOTES

Potato Ring Rot
(Howardbacteriosis infectsus)

Fig.1 Something of the blight

The most virulent bug ever to attack the variety 'Spud-u-don't-like' was introduced this week to the left-of-field crop. The potato gets it in the neck from this pernicious Transylvanian destroyer which, if unchecked, proceeds to run rings round it.

Blairus spud-u-don't-likeus

15 xi 03
Peter Brookes

Fig.2

Remedial action: stake and chips.

George Bush pays a controversial state visit to the UK. He is treated to lunch at Downing Street prepared by Nigella Lawson. However the President omits to thank Tony Blair for his support in the war in Iraq. Neither does he agree to abandon protectionist measures on steel, or give any guarantee to free British prisoners in Guantanamo Bay.

'We got him.' Saddam Hussein is finally found in a hole in the ground near his home town of Tikrit. George Bush says the ex-Iraqi leader should pay the 'ultimate penalty' for his crime.

The Hutton Inquiry is published and is deeply critical of the BBC. The Chairman Gavyn Davies and Director General Greg Dyke resign. The Corporation is declared 'in crisis'.

NATURE NOTES

Beebkeeping the Blair Way
or how to give yourself a powerful buzz.

Tony Blair says he was unaware when he urged MPs to vote for war that the allusion in the September 2002 dossier to Iraq's ability to unleash WMD in 45 minutes referred in fact to battlefield weapons. He stands by his decision to join the US in invading Iraq, emphasising to MPs that the Hutton report has cleared the government of 'sexing up' its Iraq dossier.

Clare Short alleges that British spies were instructed to carry out operations within the United Nations on officials such as Secretary General Kofi Annan, including bugging their phones. She also revisits the question of the legality of the war and whether the government had to pressure the Attorney General to give his authority for it.

NATURE NOTES

Assassin Bug
(Clareshorta vendetta)

Belly-crawling in a spooky, dark and dangerous underworld, an assassin bug seeks to ambush its prey, pick holes in it, and to suck the very life-blood from it. *(see Fig: 2)*

Fig.1 Don't let the buggers get you down.

Fig.2 Gulping gloop.

The government is poised to announce that, five years after the start of a national debate, GM crops can – on certain conditions – be grown commercially in Britain.

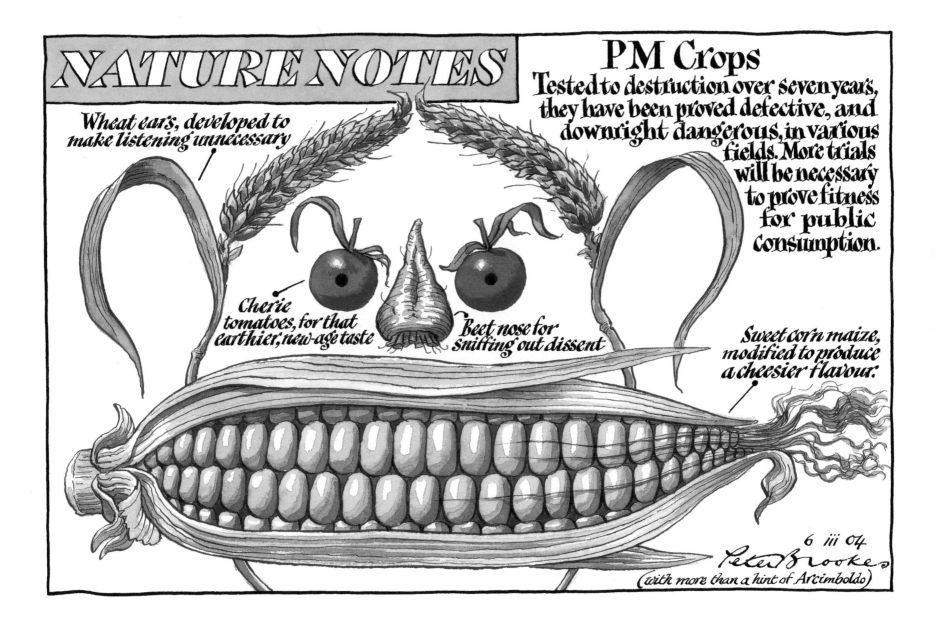

Tony Blair shakes hands with Libya's Colonel Gaddafi at the start of historic talks in Tripoli. He says that Gaddafi is willing to join the fight against terrorism, and that people should not forget the past, but move beyond it.

Immigration minister Beverley Hughes steps down in the wake of allegations about checks on migrants being waived after a backlog of cases has built up. The Home Office subsequently confirms that Hughes approved a fast-track immigration process for thousands of foreigners applying for British passports. Her resignation, repeatedly insisted upon by Opposition leader Michael Howard, is a blow for David Blunkett.

Ten countries from Eastern Europe are welcomed into the European Union at midnight on 1 May. But as Cyprus, the Czech Republic, Estonia, Hungary, Latvia, Lithuania, Malta, Poland, Slovakia and Slovenia look forward to the benefits of membership, an opinion poll suggests the French are among the most doubtful about the benefits of the expansion of the EU.